the Conservation and repair of bells and bellframes

Code of Practice

Other titles published for the Council for the Care of Churches by Church House Publishing:

Church Extensions and Adaptations, 2nd edition

Church Lighting by Peter Jay and Bill Crawforth

The Churchyards Handbook, 6th edition

A Guide to Church Inspection and Repair, 2nd edition

Historic Organ Conservation

Sounds Good: A Guide to Church Organs for Incumbents, Churchwardens and PCCs by John Norman and Jim Berrow

A Stitch in Time: Guidelines for the Care of Textiles

Stonework: Maintenance and Surface Repair by Alban Caroe and Martin Caroe, 2nd edition

Towards the Conservation and Restoration of Historic Organs

the Conservation and repair of bells and bellframes

Code of Practice

CHURCH HOUSE PUBLISHING

Church House Publishing
Church House
Great Smith Street
London SW1P 3NZ

ISBN 0 7151 7599 8

Published 1993 for the Council
of the Care of Churches
by Church House Publishing
Reset 2002

Copyright © The Central
Board of Finance of the
Church of England 1993
Copyright assigned to the
Archbishops' Council 2002

Typeset in 9.5/11 Sabon
Printed by Halstan & Co. Ltd.,
Amersham , Bucks

All rights reserved. No part of this
publication may be reproduced
or stored or transmitted by any
means or in any form, electronic
or mechanical, including
photocopying, recording, or any
information storage and retrieval
system, without written permission
which should be sought from
the Copyright and Contracts
Administrator, The Archbishops'
Council, Church House, Great
Smith Street, London SWIP 3NZ.

Tel: 020 7898 1557;
Fax: 020 7898 1449;
Email: copyright@c-of-e.org.uk

Contents

List of illustrations	vi
Foreword	vii
Introduction	1
Scope and aims	1
Statement of principles: historic bells, bellframes, and fittings	2
Specialist advice and procedure	5
Advice	5
Procedure	6
Bells worthy of preservation	6
Cast-in crown staple stumps	7
Turning worn bells	8
Chime hammers	8
Clocks and tune-playing machines	9
Recasting and replacement	9
Welding cracked and worn bells	10
Tuning	10
Canons	11
Appropriate methods of hanging	11
The augmentation of rings of bells	12
Conservation in use	12
Towers with bells hung for full-circle ringing	13
Bellframes	13
Structural evaluation	14
The conservation of bellframes of historical importance	15
The repair of timber bellframes	16
Safety	16
Documentation	16
Acoustics	17
Imitations	17
appendix 1 Assessment of bells and bellframes	18
Unlisted bells description	18
Qualitative considerations	19
Guidelines regarding the augmentation of rings	19

Historical evaluation of bellframes	20
appendix 2 Handbells	21
appendix 3 Peal boards and ringing relics	22
appendix 4 The repair of timber bellframes	23
appendix 5 Bells in redundant churches	25
appendix 6 Security of disused bells	26
appendix 7 Broken bells	27
appendix 8 Sources of grant aid	28
Index	31

Illustrations

fig. 1 Diagram of a bell and fittings	2
fig. 2 Early seventeenth-century bell with ornate inscription	3
fig. 3 Typical crown-staple crack	7
fig. 4 Steel canon-retaining headstock	11
fig. 5 Fourteenth-century frame with later long heads	13
fig. 6 Short-headed queenpost frame	14
fig. 7 Inscribed frame	15
fig. 8 Diagram of a typical timber bellframe	23
fig. 9 Diagram of a timber bellframe with pre-Reformation features	24

Foreword

I am delighted to introduce this Code of Practice which enhances and supersedes the former Code issued by the Council in 1981. A Code of Practice is of course an advisory document, not a piece of legislation, and so its provisions are best kept clear and brief. It is not intended to cover every eventuality in every case, which would be an impossible task in such a richly individual field as bells.

We owe a great debt to the Working Party which has spent long hours preparing the text. We are also grateful for the care with which other bodies have studied the result, notably English Heritage, the Central Council of Church Bell Ringers, and the bellfounders and bellhangers. I hope that this Code will form a valuable tool for all those who care for our unique heritage of bells and bellringing.

We wish to thank Mr Christopher Dalton for his permission to reproduce the photographs in this booklet.

The Very Reverend Christopher Campling, Dean of Ripon
Chairman, Council for the Care of Churches, 1988–1994

Note on the reprinted edition, 2002
The advice given in the 1993 Code of Practice remains unchanged in this reprinted edition but minor changes have been made to ensure that the text is up to date.

Introduction

Scope and aims

This Code is issued by the Council for the Care of Churches (a permanent Commission of the General Synod of the Church of England) and has been prepared by a joint working party of representatives of the Council's Bells Committee, the Central Council of Church Bell Ringers, English Heritage, and the bellfounders and bellhangers. The Code carries the endorsement of these bodies. It supersedes the Code of Practice for the Conservation of Bells and Bellframes issued by the Council for the Care of Churches in 1981.

The aims of this Code are:

(a) to encourage the continuing use of church bells to announce public worship;

(b) to ensure the conservation of historic bells, bellframes, and fittings;

(c) to encourage the art and craft of bellfounding in England;

(d) to promote the tradition of change ringing, itself an important part of the nation's heritage;

(e) to provide workable guidelines, recognizing all viewpoints and interests, and balancing the needs of conservation and bellringing practice.

Statement of principles: historic bells, bellframes, and fittings

Each case should be decided on its merits, without inflexible rules or standard specifications but being guided by the principles in this Code.

Bells and bellframes differ from most other categories of church furnishings and fittings in that, in addition to being musical instruments, they are machines. Bellframes are used to transmit large forces and are subject to dynamic loads, and bells and fittings are subject to mechanical wear. To maintain them in use, it is not enough merely to attempt to restrain the processes of

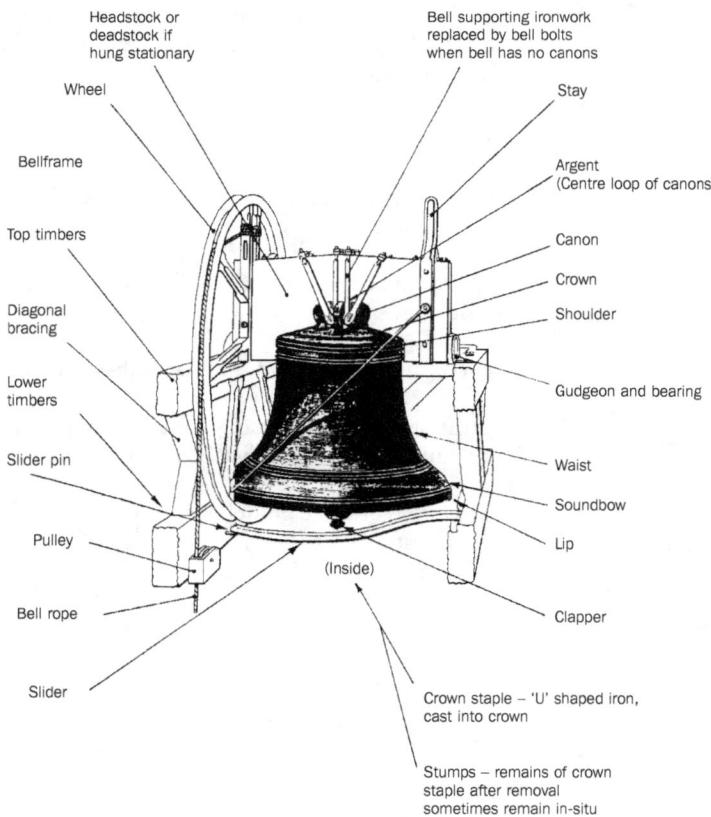

fig. 1
Diagram of a bell and fittings

fig. 2
Early seventeenth-century bell with ornate inscription, cast by Newcombe of Leicester (St Mary's Church, Astley, Warwickshire)

decay, as with most other objects; conservation must allow for continuing mechanical wear and tear. The term conservation is used to cover this sympathetic process in preference to the more inflexible term preservation.

Continuity in use is desirable: unnecessary replacement or alteration of historic bells and bellframes should be avoided. This minimum alteration philosophy should also apply to the treatment of earlier repairs and alterations. Wherever possible there should be a presumption in favour of their retention but if, after a full assessment, major replacement and alteration appear inevitable, then in such cases consideration must be given to preservation, in situ or elsewhere.

With historic bells, the presumption should be to leave as found. Any proposal to make alterations, such as the removal of canons and argent, changing the hanging method, tuning, or the drilling of holes, should be justified, particularly if in conflict with any of the criteria given in this Code, as reversibility is rarely possible.

In any proposed work of repair, an understanding and analysis of current defects are essential. The investigation of defects, together with possible remedies, should form part of the report. On completion of any work, monitoring and maintenance should form part of the normal care and inspection of the building and, together with any further reports, should be included in the church log book.

Appropriate documentation is an important aspect of any work and has a number of functions. It is part of the archaeological process and is essential to an understanding of the historical development of the bellframe and bells – a prerequisite of intelligent repair.

The following sections state criteria which will help to distinguish those bells and bellframes meriting full protection from those that do not.

Specialist advice and procedure

Advice

A Parochial Church Council (PCC) wishing to carry out work to towers, bells, fittings, or bellframes will require specialist advice. This is available from the following sources:

(a) the Diocesan Advisory Committee (DAC) and in particular its Bells Adviser;

(b) the principal bellfounders and bellhangers who have a wealth of experience in the practicalities of all work relating to bells;

(c) the Bells and Clocks specialist Committee of the Council for the Care of Churches (CCC), which can give information on the historical importance of bells, bellframes, and fittings, and their conservation, and can advise on technical problems;

(d) the Towers and Belfries Committee of the Central Council of Church Bell Ringers (CCCBR);

(e) the parish's inspecting architect;

(f) the local ringing guild or association;

(g) English Heritage (EH).

Addresses may be obtained from the CCC. It is expected that these bodies will be able to respond to a written request for advice within two months.

Work on bells or bellframes involves many different areas of expertise: the bellfounder, the bellhanger, the bellringer, the builder, the Diocesan Bells Adviser, the historian, the archaeologist, the architect, the structural engineer, and so on. Each has his or her own specialist knowledge and, on occasions, advice may conflict. This Code is intended to reconcile any differing views.

Procedure

Any work on towers, bells, bellframes, or bell fittings is likely to require a faculty. This is a permissive document granted by the consistory court of the diocese. Application forms for faculty permission are available from the Diocesan Registrar. The Chancellor (the judge of the consistory court) will require the views of the DAC and its Bells Adviser, so early contact with the Adviser is essential. It must be emphasized that although the Adviser will often recommend a scheme which is in accordance with this Code, compliance with it does not guarantee that the Chancellor will grant a faculty. No work should begin until a faculty has been granted. The bellfounder must be informed by the parish of any special conditions attached to the faculty. If variations or further work become necessary once work has begun, approval for these must similarly be obtained.

Any conditions, either long- or short-term, made by grant-awarding bodies should be considered carefully before acceptance since they must be adhered to thereafter. Equally, grants that have been made in the past, even for other parts of the building, may have involved a commitment to consult the grant-making body when embarking on further works.

Bells worthy of preservation

Lists have been drawn up of bells which should be preserved because of their historical importance. The lists aim to include all bells cast before 1550, important bells of subsequent date, and a selection of complete rings of bells by one founder. Copies of the diocesan lists are held by the CCC, where they may be consulted by appointment, and by the appropriate Diocesan Bells Adviser.

The fact that a bell is not listed does not imply that it is not worthy of preservation. An assessment should always be made of its importance to determine the appropriate treatment, using the procedure in Appendix 1.

If it is concluded as a result of the assessment that the bell should not be recast, have its canons removed, or be tuned, regardless of its suitability or condition, then a recommendation should be made to the CCC that the bell should be listed.

Specialist advice and procedure

fig. 3
Typical crown-staple crack (Church of St Mary Magdalene, Sparkford, Somerset)

Cast-in crown staple stumps

Research links these with crown cracks, and concludes that it is desirable to remove as much of the iron stumps as possible to avoid future trouble.

Crown cracks due to cast-in staple stumps account for at least half of all cracks in bells. Although these cracks can now be repaired by welding, it is desirable that they do not occur in the first place. The evidence shows that, when the stumps are close together, drilling a central hole minimizes the risk of cracking. If it is assessed that very little or none of the iron can be removed by drilling a central hole, then it is recommended that the stumps be drilled out separately.

The central hole can be used for fitting an independent crown staple. This eases clappering requirements and minimizes the wear on the soundbow caused by the clapper ball sliding round the inside of the bell after striking. This often happens with worn cast-in crown staples, especially when a bell has been turned.

It is totally inadequate for the staple to be cut off flush with the inner surface of the crown of the bell without at least drilling a stress-relieving central hole.

Turning worn bells

If wear in the soundbow from the internal clapper or an external hammer reaches 10 per cent of the unworn thickness, turning the bell or moving the hammer is necessary to reduce the risk of cracking. When a bell is rehung, the clapper and any hammer should strike upon an unworn thickness of the soundbow and preferably at 45° from any welded crack.

Chime hammers

Hammers should be arranged to strike an unworn thickness of the soundbow (see above).

Any Ellacombe-type chiming apparatus should be located in the ringing chamber, with a clearly visible notice advising ringers to release the hammers before swinging the bells. In cases where the apparatus is located at a different level, a simple device should exist to preclude the possibility of the bells being chimed while being swung.

Where electric hammers are fitted, a clearly labelled override or isolator switch should be prominently positioned in the ringing chamber. A bright red light should signify that it is unsafe to swing the bells and a bright green one that it is safe to do so.

Clock and tune-playing machine hammers (see next page) should be fitted with pull-off wires and fastenings in the ringing chamber, together with a notice warning that they must be pulled clear while the bells are being swung.

Extension ropes should be fitted only to bells without clock hammers.

Tolling hammers operated from levels other than the ringing chamber should include a simple device to prevent the hammers operating when the bells are being swung.

Hammers and ropes should be arranged to minimize the chance of a bell becoming damaged as a result of excessive impact, or of damping by holding the hammer against the bell immediately after impact. The practice of connecting ropes to the flights of ringing clappers, known as 'clocking', is strongly deprecated.

Clocks and tune-playing machines

When both clocks and bells are present in towers, special care must be taken to ensure work to one does not interfere with the other. In such cases, both the Bells and the Clocks Adviser should be consulted.

Tune-playing machines present a particular problem. A number have been needlessly destroyed during work on bells. Every effort should be made to keep them and, if possible, bring them back into a usable condition. Again, advice should be sought from both specialist Advisers before any work commences.

Recasting and replacement

Listed bells should not be recast. Where a bell is damaged, welding is often a solution (see next page). If it is beyond repair, it should be preserved and a new bell provided to take its place in the ring.

Unlisted bells cast before 1700 should not be recast if welding is possible. Bells cast after 1700 may be considered for recasting only after an assessment has been made in accordance with Appendix 1.

Where a bell is to be recast, it is normal practice to reproduce all inscriptions and marks in facsimile, with the date of recasting and the founder's name or mark added.

Welding cracked and worn bells

Much progress has been made in this area in recent years, and many bells have been repaired by welding and returned to use. Current experience indicates that welding can be used effectively to:

(a) repair cracks;

(b) replace pieces missing;

(c) build up soundbow thickness in the case of uncracked bells which are so worn that further turning to allow the clapper or hammer to strike metal of full thickness is not possible.

Tuning

A set of bells should sound musical, balanced, and in tune. Bells are fixed pitch musical instruments and do not go out of tune to any great extent. Where bells are not in tune, or where they are poor tonally, careful and limited adjustments to the notes and principal harmonic tones can usually be effected. Tuning involves the removal of metal from a bell; thus tuning, or further tuning, produces a small but irreversible change in both appearance and sound. In the case of bells worthy of preservation, there is a presumption against tuning.

Tuning usually involves adjustments to all the bells within a set. Where the set consists of only three or fewer bells, tuning is rarely worthwhile.

The case for or against tuning therefore involves balancing the desirability of leaving as found on the one hand, against the potential benefits on the other.

The aim should be to conserve listed bells and other bells deemed worthy of preservation (following the assessment in Appendix 1) in as near their original state as possible. In such cases, tuning should be undertaken only when essential, even if the bells have been tuned in the past.

Canons

As a general principle, canons should not be removed. This general rule may be relaxed only if the bell is unlisted, cast after 1700 and to be hung for full-circle ringing. Particularly fine or unusual canons should be retained regardless of the bell's age, and others should be retained where it would help balance bells in a ring which includes other bells with canons.

Appropriate methods of hanging

Where canons are retained, headstocks and deadstocks should be designed so that the canons are visible. Although canons were designed to carry the whole weight of the bell, the cutting away of the cast-in crown staple and the drilling of a central hole permit the fitting of a centre bolt which will carry much of the bell's weight. Additional support should be provided by metalwork designed to support the bell by its canons, although bell bolts may be used where holes already exist, or where the bell is unlisted and cast after 1800.

fig. 4
Steel canon-retaining headstock. The bell has been quarter-turned. (St Peter's Church, Mancetter, Warwickshire)

Where fewer than six canons remain and there are no holes through the crown, 'U' bolts may be fitted around the surviving canons and that part of the deadstock or headstock over the stumps of the broken canons extended to butt on to the crown.

Where a bell is hung for full-circle ringing, the loads on the canons are some four times greater than with one hung stationary. For this reason, bolts may be used regardless of a bell's age. Existing holes should be used to avoid or minimize the drilling of new ones.

Where bells have weak crowns, steps should be taken to spread the loads from the bell bolts over a wide area to minimize local stressing. For example, a resin pad may be cast on to the inside of the crown and extra large washers used under the heads of bell bolts.

The augmentation of rings of bells

The purpose of increasing the number of bells within a set is to make possible a greater variety of tunes or changes. When the opportunity for augmentation of a ring arises, there are important considerations to be taken into account as well as assessing the need to preserve existing bells: the assessment procedure in Appendix 1, at page 19 should therefore be used.

When a ring is augmented, the additional bells should be designed or selected to match the existing bells in pitch, tone, and strength rather than the latter being altered to match the new.

Conservation in use

Some bell installations exist complete with their original fittings, so that they have survived virtually as they were 200 or more years ago. These cases require special consideration, and repairs should, as far as possible, be carried out so that identical fittings are used and the character of the installation is not lost.

Specialist advice and procedure

fig. 5
Fourteenth-century frame with later long heads (Church of St Peter and St Paul, West Newton, Norfolk)

Alternatively, it may be desirable to conserve the headstocks, securing ironwork, wheels, clappers, and other fittings in the old bellframe, and rehang the bells themselves with new fittings in a new bellframe elsewhere in the tower.

Towers with bells hung for full-circle ringing

If any modifications are suggested to a ring of bells, the parish's inspecting architect should be consulted on the ability of the tower to absorb the forces set up within the fabric.

Bellframes

Until now the study of bellframes has been a neglected field and many of historical importance have been lost. A list of historic bellframes is being prepared and it is hoped that it will be available for consultation at the CCC. However, in many cases, on the spot assessment will be necessary and this should be made as set out in Appendix 1, at page 20. Where assistance is required on the assessment, advice can be obtained through the CCC.

fig. 6
Short-headed queenpost frame (All Saints' Church, Knipton, Leicestershire)

Structural evaluation

Bellframes for bells not to be hung for full-circle ringing include many of historical importance. Since the loads to be carried are generally quite small, first consideration should be given to repair (see p. 16).

Where the bells are to be hung for full-circle ringing, the bellframe will carry large dynamic forces. Excessive movement will make the bells difficult to handle and may cause considerable damage, not only to the bellframe itself but to the ringing fittings and to the tower. The repair of the existing bellframe should always be considered and a schedule of essential structural work prepared to assist in comparisons of costed options and, for historically important bellframes, consideration be given to how much original timber can be retained for use.

Specialist advice and procedure

fig. 7
Inscribed frame
(St Michael's Church, Onibury, Shropshire)

The conservation of bellframes of historical importance
Wherever possible, a historic bellframe should be retained in use. Where this is not possible, consideration should be given either to retaining the original bellframe in situ with a new bellframe lower in the tower or to removing it elsewhere. When retained in situ, some of the floorboards at bellframe level will need to be removed to allow sufficient sound to pass through. If this is done around the edges, it will enhance ventilation to beam ends.

Other options range from hoisting the old bellframe to a higher level in the tower, to preserving a representative sideframe fixed to one of the internal tower walls. The old bellframe should be kept free from accumulated debris, dry, and well ventilated, and only minimal structural repairs should be carried out. Since these options destroy archaeological evidence, recording will be necessary before removal. PCCs should investigate how this work might be carried out and funded. Drawings should be supplemented by a written report which covers the features of the bellframe, such as re-use, alteration, and adaptation. The record should be made by a suitably qualified person.

The repair of timber bellframes

The aim is to arrest further decay and carry out sufficient repairs to achieve a structure capable of carrying the dynamic forces imposed on it whilst conserving as much of the original timber as possible. The extent of repairs may need to be much greater in the case of bells hung for full-circle ringing than for chiming.

An accurate record survey of the bellframe is an essential starting point. From this, the condition can be marked and contract drawings for repairs set out. Some general guidelines are given in Appendix 4. Specific repair options can be obtained from the CCC and the treatment of woodwork is discussed in the CCCBR Handbook, Towers and Bells.

Safety

Safety in belfries is an important matter and PCCs are advised to study the CCCBR Handbook, Towers and Bells.

Documentation

In general, recording will be by measured drawings, a written description, and photographs; it should also include a full digital tonal analysis of the bells, preferably supplemented by an audio recording. Reports on bell installations should give details of the date and founder of each bell in the ring, the approximate age of the bellframe and fittings, and any other points of special interest. This information should accompany the faculty application papers.

All work undertaken to bells or bellframes should be recorded in the church log book. Drawings of old bellframes which have to be replaced should be kept with the log book and a copy lodged in the Diocesan Record Office.

Details of bells (including handbells), bellframes, peal boards, and any ringing relics that belong to the church should be included in the inventory.

Acoustics

Special attention should be given to acoustics, both internal and external, when the position of a bellframe is changed in the tower.

The question of the control of sound within the immediate vicinity of the tower should be dealt with by the church architect who can obtain advice from the CCC.

Imitations

Mechanical, electrical, or electronic imitations of bells are strongly deprecated.

appendix 1
Assessment of bells and bellframes

Unlisted bells description

The following factual technical information should be established and documented:

(a) the position of the bell in the ring;

(b) the identity of its founder;

(c) the date of casting;

(d) its diameter (across the mouth of the bell)

(e) its weight;

(f) its strike-note and, if possible, the principal harmonics;

(g) its scale of thickness;

(h) whether the bell is sound or, if cracked, the extent and possible cause of any crack;

(i) the overall casting quality;

(j) the detail and overall quality of inscriptions, special features, and the shape and position of moulding wires;

(k) whether it has canons and argent, their condition, and any special features;

(l) whether the bell has been drilled and to what extent;

(m) whether the bell has been tuned and to what extent;

(n) whether the bell has been turned;

(o) the extent of clapper and hammer indentations;

(p) whether it retains its cast-in crown staple.

Qualitative considerations

(a) is the bell historically noteworthy locally or nationally?

(b) with reference to its date, style and size, is the bell an important or rare example of the founder's work?

(c) is the bell unusually fine in tone and tune?

(d) does the combination of shape, quality of casting, inscriptions, and canons create a bell of particularly fine appearance?

(e) does the bell relate in size, pitch, tone, and style to the other bells in the set?

(f) are there any features other than those listed above which make the bell noteworthy?

Guidelines regarding the augmentation of rings

(a) is there enough space for any proposed additional bell, its hanging, its equipment, access to it, and space for the bellringer?

(b) can the tower safely and rigidly support an additional load?

(c) has the means of sound dispersal been considered?

(d) will the mechanical performance be satisfactory?

Historical evaluation of bellframes

(a) of what materials is the bellframe constructed?

(b) how old is the bellframe?

(c) is it by an identifiable maker, and what is the documentary evidence?

(d) is it a rare example of the maker's work, or has it especial value as an example of bellframe evolution?

(e) is it completely original or does it provide evidence of the evolution of the ring?

(f) how was the bell rung originally?

(g) does it incorporate pre-Reformation features, such as curved side frame braces, king posts, or short heads (even when incorporated in a later bellframe)?

(h) what is the quality of workmanship?

appendix 2
Handbells

Handbells date from the eighteenth century onwards, and early examples are worthy of conservation. They should be handled with care; bell metal is brittle and easily cracked. They should be kept in a secure, clean, and dry place, ideally in a box specially made for them.

appendix 3
Peal boards and ringing relics

Peal boards and ringing relics such as ringers' rules, beer jugs, and number boards are a part of the heritage of bellringing and should be protected and preserved. Advice can be sought from the CCC on their conservation and grants may be available towards the cost of such work.

Written archive material (such as belfry meeting minutes, accounts, peal books) should be preserved. Items over 100 years old should be deposited in the Diocesan Record Office or other suitable repository, or, where the parish has the necessary exemption to retain ancient records, in the record cabinet.

appendix 4
The repair of timber bellframes

Before a suitable strategy can be chosen, the bellframe, including the foundation beams supporting it, should be assessed for structural adequacy. It is possible that a frame carrying bells for full-circle ringing may need additional foundation beams so that vertical deflection is reduced and horizontal forces are distributed between all four tower walls.

The extent of repair should be considered before deciding technique. If the bellframe needs to be partly dismantled (perhaps to replace a decayed cill), this will allow foundation beam ends to be repaired from above as well as from below.

When analysing the bellframe, it is only by ringing the bells that movement can be observed.

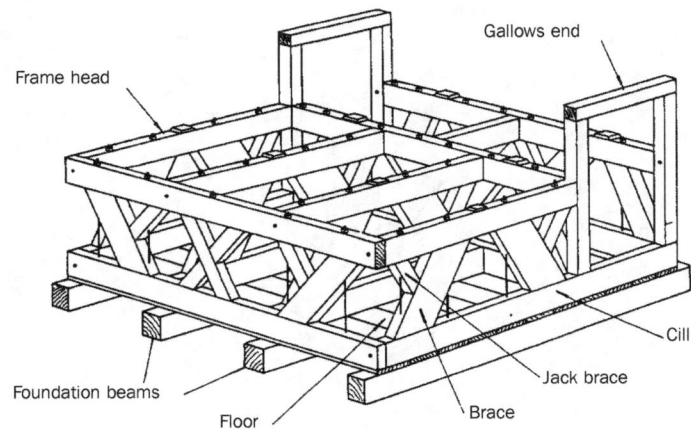

fig. 8 A typical timber bellframe

appendix 4

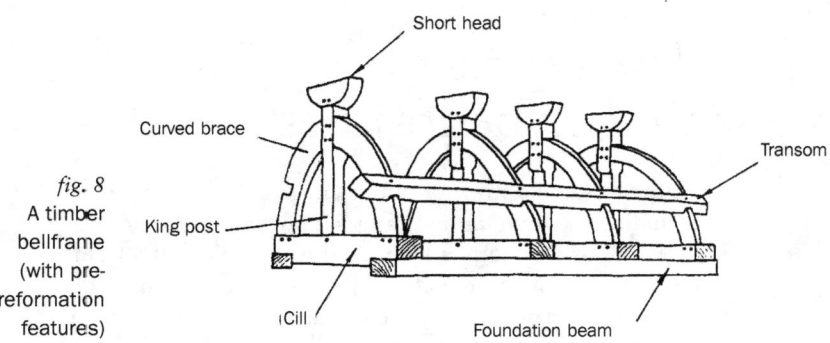

fig. 8
A timber bellframe (with pre-reformation features)

appendix 5
Bells in redundant churches

Some redundant churches retain their bells. Those likely to be demolished or converted to secular use normally have their bells removed and securely stored as soon as the future use of the fabric is determined. From the date set in the Pastoral Scheme for the declaration of redundancy until the making of a redundancy scheme (the 'waiting period'), the safety of the bells is the responsibility of the Diocesan Board of Finance. That Board and the Diocesan Redundant Churches Uses Committee (through the appropriate Redundant Churches Furnishings Officer) should liaise with the Diocesan Bells Adviser to ensure that the bell installation and tower furniture, as a whole, are kept intact, to ensure their satisfactory maintenance and security, and to find a suitable future.

Any proposal should ensure that bells which are listed for preservation in redundant churches will be preserved complete, either for use or in a museum, and that the Board's prior approval in principle is obtained so that the proposal may be effected as soon as possible after the scheme has been made. The Advisory Board for Redundant Churches should also be consulted. Complete rings may be moved to other churches, and every effort should be made to retain their integrity. Faculty application for such installation should consider the future of any existing bell installation in the recipient church.

Where, in exceptional cases, it is considered essential to remove the bells from a church declared redundant, but awaiting the making of a redundancy scheme, the Pastoral Measure 1983 requires the normal faculty procedure.

The Central Council of Church Bell Ringers has a Committee and a Rescue Fund for Redundant Bells.

appendix 6
Security of disused bells

In England during the 25-year period to 1990, many bells were stolen, ranging in casting date from c.1275 to modern times, some weighing over half a ton. Few have been recovered. Disused bells are very vulnerable to theft, particularly when left in the body of the church, and it may be appropriate to deposit them in a museum on indefinite loan. Alternatively, they should be preserved in the tower, near the other bells, no lower than the first floor. Wherever possible, disused bells should be returned to use.

appendix 7
Broken bells

Some bells, including those recovered following theft, have been broken to pieces. It may be possible to use modern adhesives in the reassembly of a bell worthy of preservation.

appendix 8
Sources of grant aid

Council for the Care of Churches
The Conservation Officer
Council for the Care of Churches
Church House
Great Smith Street
London
SW1P 3NZ

Tel: 020 7898 1866

Grants, from funds made available by various charitable trusts, are given for the conservation of bells and bellframes of historical significance. The CCC also publishes a booklet called *Fundraising for Your Church Building* which is available from Church House Bookshop (Tel: 020 7898 1306) or on-line at www.churchcare.co.uk

Central Council of Church Bell Ringers
Bell Restoration Funds Committee
c/o Mrs Kate Flavell
7 Kings Avenue
New Malden
Surrey
KT3 4DX
www.cccbr.org.uk/committees/brfc/brfc.html

The terms of reference of the Committee are to promote the restoration of bells, by investigating and disseminating information on fund raising, charitable status, tax-efficient giving and sympathetic Trusts. The Committee also makes recommendations to the Trustees of The Manifold Trust. Emphasis is on the restoration of bells which have been unringable for some time.

English Heritage
23 Savile Row
London
W1X 1AB

English Heritage and the Heritage Lottery Fund run a joint scheme for 'Repair Grants for Places of Worship in England 2002-2005', the main focus of which is to support urgent repair work which keeps the main fabric structurally stable and watertight. It is unlikely that the conservation of bellframes would be a high priority for a grant under this scheme, and work to bells would not qualify. Projects involving both the conservation of bellframes and/or of bells might qualify under the Heritage Lottery Fund's 'Your Heritage' grant scheme, but they would have to give people a better opportunity to experience heritage by improving access and be of demonstrable wider community and public benefit.

The Barron Bell Trust
The Managing Trustees
71 Lower Green Road
Pembury
Tunbridge Wells
Kent
TN2 4EB

This is a charitable fund for 'providing, installing, inspecting, replacing, or maintaining' bells in churches where 'in the opinion of the Trustees the associations are low as distinguished from high, broad, or modernist'.

The Leche Trust
84 Cicada Road
London
SW18 2NZ

This Trust gives grants for the conservation of bells cast during the Georgian period.

The Sharpe Trust
The Grant Secretary
The Old Bakehouse
Beech Pike
Elkstone
Cheltenham
Glos.
GL53 9PL

Grants are made for the repair and restoration of bells in England and Wales (only).

Diocesan and County Guilds of Bellringers

These guilds of bellringers may be able to offer grants, or to assist with voluntary labour, thereby reducing the cost of a scheme. Addresses are obtainable from the Diocesan Bells Adviser or from the CCCBR.

Index

acoustics 17
Advisory Board for Redundant Churches 25
architects 5, 13
archive material, preservation of 22
argent, removal of 3

Barron Bell Trust, The 29
Bell Ringers, Central Council of Church 5, 25, 28
Bell Ringers, Diocesan and County Guilds of 5, 30
bellframes
 assessment of 13, 18–19
 conservation of 2–4
 historical evaluation of 14–16, 20
 listed 2–4, 13
 repair of 14, 16, 23–24
bells
 assessment of 18–19
 augmentation of rings 12, 19
 broken, reassembly of 27
 conservation of 2–4, 10, 12–13
 disused, and security 26
 full-circle ringing 11, 13, 14, 16, 23
 historical importance of 3, 6, 14, 15, 16
 imitations 17
 listed 6, 9, 11, 25
 recasting 9
 in redundant churches 25
 replacement 9
 tonal analysis 16
 turning worn 8
Bells Adviser 5, 6, 25
bolts, fitting of 11, 12

canons 3, 11
cast-in crown staple 7–8
CCC *see* Council for the Care of Churches
Central Council of Church Bell Ringers (CCCBR) 5, 16, 25, 28
chime hammers 8–9
clappers 7, 13
clock hammers 8

clocking 9
clocks 9
conservation 3, 10, 12–13
continuity in use 3
Council for the Care of Churches (CCC) 6, 13, 22, 28
cracks
 crown-staple 6, 7
 welding of 10
crown staple, cast-in 7–8, 11

deadstocks 11
Diocesan Advisory Committee for the Care of Churches (DAC) 5, 6
Diocesan and County Guilds of Bell Ringers 5, 30
disused bells and security 26
documentation 4, 16–17

electric hammers 8
Ellacombe-type chiming apparatus 8
English Heritage 5, 29

faculty permission 6
full-circle ringing 11, 13, 14, 16, 23

grants 6, 22, 28–30

hammers 8, 9
handbells 17, 21
hanging methods 3, 11–12
headstocks 11, 12
historic bells 3
historical evaluation of bellframes 14–16, 20
historical importance of bells 3, 6, 14, 15, 16
hole drilling 3, 7, 11

imitations 17
inscriptions 3, 9
inventory 3–4, 16, 17
iron stumps 7–8

Leche Trust, The 29
listed bells 6, 9, 11, 25

31

Index

marks, reproduction of 9

peal boards 17, 22
preservation 6, 25

recasting 9
redundant churches, bells in 25
rehanging 12
relics, ringing 17, 22
repairs, welding 10
replacement 9
Rescue Fund for Redundant Bells 25
ringing guild 5, 30
ringing relics 17, 22
rings
  augmentation of 12, 19
  transfer of 25

safety considerations 16
Sharpe Trust, The 30
sound control 17, 19
soundbow 10
specialist advice 5–6
structural evaluation 14
stumps, removal of 7–8

tolling hammers 9
tonal analysis, digital 17
Towers and Belfries Committee 5, 16
tune-playing machines 9
tuning 3, 10

welding 7, 10
worn bells, turning 8

www.ingramcontent.com/pod-product-compliance
Lightning Source LLC
Chambersburg PA
CBHW072115290426
44110CB00014B/1927